THE AGRICOLA & GERMANIA

PUBLIUS CORNELIUS TACITUS

A Translation into English by

A. S. KLINE

Published with Selected Illustrations

POETRY IN TRANSLATION
www.poetryintranslation.com

Please direct sales or editorial enquiries to:
tonykline@poetryintranslation.com

This print edition is published by
Poetry In Translation (*www.poetryintranslation.com*),
via On-Demand Publishing LLC, (a Delaware limited liability Company that does business under the name "CreateSpace") in partnership with
Amazon Services UK Limited (a UK limited company with registration number 03223028 and its registered office at 60 Holborn Viaduct, London, Greater London, EC1A 2BN, UK)
ISBN-10: 1517250862
ISBN-13: 978-1517250867

CONTENTS

AGRICOLA

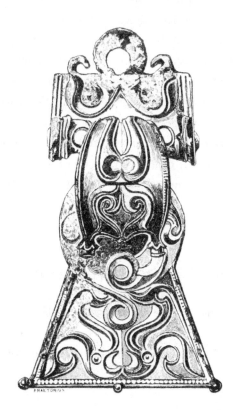

'Bronze Gilt Broach. Aesica, Northumberland'

An Introduction to the Study of Prehistoric Art

Ernest Albert Parkyn (p366, 1915)

Internet Archive Book Images

SECTION 1: ON BIOGRAPHY AND AUTO-BIOGRAPHY

It was a custom in the past not yet relinquished by our own age, indifferent though we may now be to events, to relay to posterity the deeds and manners of famous men; whenever, that is, mighty and noble virtue had conquered and suppressed that vice common to all states, great and small, the ignorance and envy of what is good.

And just as, in our predecessors' times, the age was more favourable and open to actions worth recording, so distinguished men of ability were led to produce those records of virtue, not to curry favour or from ambition, but for the reward of a good conscience. Many indeed considered it rather a matter of self-respect than arrogance to recount their own lives, and a Rutilius Rufus or an Aemilius Scaurus could do so without scepticism or disparagement; virtue indeed being most esteemed in those ages which give birth to it most readily. But in this day and age, though I set out to write the life of one already dead, I am forced to seek the indulgence which an attack upon him would not require, so savage is the spirit of these times, and hostile to virtue.

SECTION 2: THE BURNING OF THE BOOKS

We read that Rusticus the Stoic's praise of Thrasea, and Senecio's of Priscus were declared a capital offence, so that not only the authors themselves but their books were condemned, and the works of our greatest men assigned to the flames, in the heart of the Forum, on the orders of the triumvirs.

Perhaps it was thought that the voice of the people, the freedom of the Senate, and the conscience of mankind would vanish in those flames, since the teachers of knowledge were also expelled and all moral excellence exiled, so that virtue might be nowhere encountered.

Indeed we have given signal proof of our subservience; and just as former ages saw the extremes of liberty, so ours those of servitude, robbed by informants of even the ears and tongue of conversation. We would have lost memory itself as well as speech if to forget were as easy as to be silent.

SECTION 3: THE REVIVAL

Now at last our spirits revive; at the birth of this blessed age, the Emperor Nerva at once joined things long disassociated, power and liberty, while Trajan daily adds to the felicities of our times, so that the public has not merely learned to hope and pray with confidence, but has gained assurance as to the fulfilment of its prayers, and strength. Though it is still in the nature of human frailty that the remedy acts more slowly than the disease, and just as the body is slow to grow, swift to decay, so it is easier to destroy wit and enthusiasm than it is to revive them, while inertia has a certain charm, and the apathy we hate at first we later love.

During the space of fifteen years, a large part of a lifetime, change on change did for many, the Emperor's savagery for others, they being the most resolute: while we few who remain have outlived, so to speak, not merely our neighbours, but ourselves; since those years were stolen from our prime of life, while youths reached age, and old men the very edge of the grave, in silence.

Even though my speech is hoarse and unpractised, I shall not hesitate to compose a record of our former slavery, and our present blessings. In the meantime this work's intention is to honour Agricola, my father-in-law: and it will be commended for, or at least excused by, its profession of filial affection.

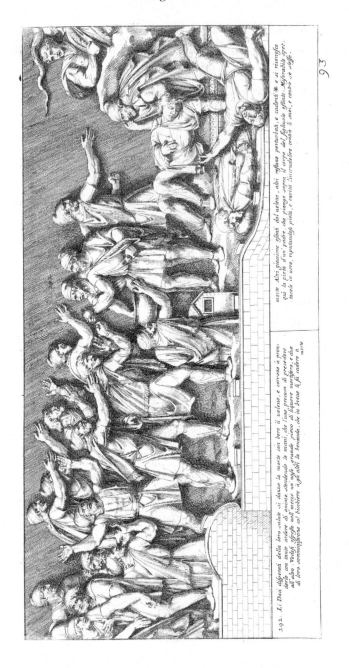

'A Portion of the Trajan Column's Spiral Relief'
Pietro Santi Bartoli (Italian, 1635 – 1700)
The Getty's Open Content Program

SECTION 4: AGRICOLA'S BOYHOOD AND YOUTH

Gnaeus Julius Agricola was born in the ancient and illustrious colony of Forum Julii (Fréjus), and his grandfathers were both Imperial procurators, a noble equestrian office. Julius Graecinus, his father, was a Senator noted for his pursuit of rhetoric and philosophy; the very virtues which earned for him Caligula's anger; ordered to prosecute Marcus Silanus he refused and was put to death. His mother was Julia Procilla, a woman of rare rectitude. Raised in her loving care he spent his boyhood and youth cultivating all the civilised accomplishments. He was protected from any temptation towards wrongdoing not only by his own sound and virtuous nature but also by Massilia who provided the foundation to his studies and acted as his guide, he representing a happy mixture of Greek refinement and provincial simplicity. I remember how he used to say himself that when young he was inclined to drink more deeply of philosophy than is acceptable for a Roman and a Senator, his mother's prudence restraining his glowing passion. No doubt his noble and aspiring mind desired the beauty and splendour of great and glorious ideas with more violence than restraint. Soon age and reason calmed him, and he preserved, as is most difficult, moderation in his studies.

SECTION 5: MILITARY APPRENTICESHIP IN BRITAIN

His first military service in Britain (58-62AD) brought him to the notice of Suetonius Paulinus, a conscientious and disciplined general, who selected him for assessment as a member of his staff. Agricola was neither slapdash, in the manner of those young men who treat soldiering as a game, nor traded idly on his tribune's role and inexperience to win leave for pleasure; rather he gained knowledge of the province, made himself known to the men, learnt from the experts, followed the best, sought nothing in ostentation, but shrank from nothing in fear, behaving as one eager but cautious.

'Roman Soldier'

Pieter Romans (Jr.), 1832

The Rijksmuseum

At no time was Britain more troubled or the situation more in doubt: veterans were slaughtered, colonies burned, forces cut off from their base; one day brought victory, the next a struggle for life. Though the leadership and strategy were another's, though the high command and credit for securing the province were the general's, yet the young soldier gained skill, experience and a sense of purpose. Desire for military glory invaded his spirit, unwelcome in an age which looked unfavourably on those who distinguished themselves and where great reputation was no less a danger than ill-repute.

SECTION 6: ROME AND ASIA MINOR

From Britain he returned to Rome (62AD) to take up office; wedding Domitia Decidiana, born of an illustrious line. The marriage proved a brilliant ornament and a support to him in his career. They lived in wonderful harmony, through their mutual affection and wish to put each other first, a good wife deserving greater praise the more one finds fault with a bad one.

The chances of the quaestorship brought him Asia Minor as his province (64AD), and Salvius Titianus as his pro-consul, neither of which corrupted him, though the province was rich and open to exploitation, while the proconsul was filled with greed, and ready for anything that would buy mutual silence regarding wrongdoing. There, a daughter (Julia, later wife to Tacitus) was born to him, a help and consolation, since he lost the son he had briefly carried in his arms.

He passed the year between his quaestorship and his tribunate of the plebs in peace and quiet, as well as his year (66AD) of office, skilfully surviving Nero's reign (54-68AD), when it was wise to remain passive. His praestorship (68AD) followed the same even tenor; no judicial duties falling to his lot. As for the games and other vanities of office, he held the mean between lavishness and thrift, far from extravagance on the one hand, closer to public opinion on the other. Chosen by Galba (June 68AD) to take an inventory of temple treasures his diligent inquiries showed that the

State judged there to have been no sacrilege other than that perpetrated by Nero.

SECTION 7: RETURN TO BRITAIN

The following year (69AD – The Year of the Four Emperors) dealt his home and peace of mind a heavy blow. For Otho's navy, hostile and roving freely, while looting Intimilium (Ventimiglia) in Liguria, murdered Agricola's mother on her estate, plundering the estate and a large part of his inheritance, that being the motive for the murder. While proceeding to carry out the solemn rites, Agricola heard the news that Vespasian aspired to power, and at once joined his party.

Mucianus initiated the new reign and ran affairs in Rome, Domitian being very young and simply enjoying free use of his father's wealth. Mucianus sent Agricola to levy soldiers and, as he showed energy and loyalty, appointed him to Britain, to command the Twentieth Legion (Valeria Victrix), which had been slow to transfer its allegiance, his predecessor (Coelius), it was said, having behaved mutinously: indeed the fearsome legion had proved too much even for consular command, such that the praetorian commander had no power to restrain them, whether due to his or the soldiers' character. Agricola, both successor and judge, with rare leniency preferred it known that he found the men loyal, rather than forcing them to behave so.

'A Roman Legion'
Marco Dente (Italian, c. 1493 – 1527)
National Gallery of Art | NGA Images

SECTION 8: SERVICE UNDER PETILIUS CERIALIS

Vettius Bolanus was then a milder governor of Britain than a troublesome province requires, and Agricola, being skilled in diplomacy and used to blending his sense of honour with that of expediency, tempered his own ardour, and restrained his enthusiasm, lest it become over-strong. Shortly thereafter (71AD), Britain received Petilius Cerialis as governor, and Agricola's virtues found scope for display. Though at first Cerialis only offered him effort and risk, he later granted him his portion of glory, often allowing him a share of command to test him, sometimes increasing his allotted forces based on success. Agricola never vaunted his actions to augment his own credit. He attributed his good fortune, as the inferior, to his leader and commander. So by virtue of his deference, and his reluctance to put himself forward, he escaped others envy without lacking distinction.

SECTION 9: GOVERNORSHIP OF GALLIA AQUITANIA

On returning from command of his legion, Vespasian, since deified, enrolled him among the patricians, and granted him governorship of Gallia Aquitania (73AD), an especially significant role both administratively and as a promise of the consulship for which he was destined.

Many imagine that the soldier's mind lacks subtlety, since his jurisdiction in camp is assured and dealings there are heavy-handed, without the need for legal skills. Thanks to his native shrewdness, Agricola, though among civilians, dealt with them readily and justly. His official duties and his hours of relaxation were carefully partitioned: when judicial business required it, he was serious, focused and severe, yet more often merciful; when the demands of office had been satisfied there was no further show of power; he eschewed moroseness, arrogance and greed. With him, as is most rare, an easy manner did not serve to diminish his authority nor his severity affection. To refer to the honesty and restraint of such a man is almost to insult virtue itself. Fame which even good men often covet, he never sought, neither by parading his virtues, nor by practising intrigue: incapable of fuelling rivalry with colleagues nor contending with the agents of empire, he thought it inglorious to succeed so, and sordid to be thus contaminated.

He was retained for less than three years in Aquitania, and then recalled with hopes of an immediate consulship, to an accompanying rumour that Britain would be granted him as his province, not that he ever spoke of it, but simply because he seemed suitable. Rumour is not always in error; sometimes it even determines the choice. The consul (suffectus, 77AD) betrothed his daughter Julia, a girl of great promise, to me, then a mere youth, and on conclusion of his office gave her to me in marriage. He was posted immediately thereafter to Britain, and also appointed to the high priesthood.

SECTION 10: GOVERNORSHIP OF BRITAIN: ITS GEOGRAPHY

Britain's location and inhabitants having been attested to by many writers, I reproduce them here not as a challenge to their efforts or talent but because Agricola first conquered the island completely. Where earlier writers embellished with rhetoric what was not yet fully discovered, here facts will be faithfully recorded.

'A Map of Britain in the Most Perfect State of Roman Power and Government'

The History of Great Britain: From the First Invasion of it by the Romans

Under Julius Cæsar

Robert Henry, Malcolm Laing, John Adams (p602, 1789)

The British Library

Britain comprises the largest island known to Rome, in extent and situation stretching over towards Germania eastwards and Hispania westwards, while to the south it is in sight of Gaul; its northern shores alone have no land facing them, but are washed by wastes of open sea. Livy the most eloquent of ancient and Fabius Rusticus of modern authors respectively likened its shape to a lengthened shoulder-blade, or a double axe-head. And this is its form as far north as Caledonia, a form which tradition extended to the whole; but travelling onwards a vast and irregular tract of land extends to the furthest shores, tapering like a wedge. Under Agricola a Roman fleet first navigated the shore of the furthest sea (84AD), and confirmed Britain as an island, in the same voyage reaching the unexplored islands known as the Orcades (the Orkneys) and claiming them. Thule (Shetland?) was merely sighted, as their orders took them only thus far, and winter was approaching. But they declared the waves sluggish, resistant to the oar, and likewise unresponsive to the wind, presumably because mountainous land, the cause and origin of storms, is scarcer, and the unbroken mass of deeper water is harder to set in motion. It is not for this work to seek out the nature of the ocean and its tides, besides many have recorded them: I would only add that nowhere has the sea greater power: many currents set in all directions, the tides not merely washing the shore then ebbing, but penetrating the coastline and drowning it, even piercing the mountain chains as though deep in their own element.

SECTION II: BRITAIN'S INHABITANTS

The question of who indeed first inhabited Britain, and whether they are indigenous or newcomers, is, as usual among barbarous nations, difficult to ascertain. Their physical traits vary, and lead to speculation. The red-haired, large-limbed inhabitants of Caledonia suggest a Germanic origin; while the dark colouration of the Silures (of South Wales), their plentiful curls, and the relative position of Spain, attests to immigrant Iberians in former times, who occupied the area; again, those nearest the Gauls are like them, whether because of the enduring power of heredity, or because the common climate of two projecting lands that face each other moulds the physique. Taking the wider view, it is certainly credible that the Gauls might occupy a neighbouring island; you find the same ceremonies and religious beliefs there; their languages are not too dissimilar, they have the same recklessness in courting danger, and the same anxiety to escape it, when it comes. But the Britons are spirited, not yet emasculated by years of peace. We hear the Gauls too were once warlike: later quiet brought sluggishness, and courage and liberty were lost together. Such are the Britons who were conquered some time ago; the rest remain as the Gauls once were.

SECTION 12: THE NATURE OF THE LAND

Their strength is on foot, though certain tribes fight from chariots, the charioteer holding the place of honour, while the retainers make war. Once the people were ruled by kings, now the disputes and ambitions of minor chieftains distract them. Nor do we have a better weapon against the stronger tribes than this lack of common purpose. It is rare for two or three tribes to unite against a mutual danger; thus, fighting singly, they are universally defeated.

The weather in Britain is foul, with dense cloud and rain; but the cold is not severe. The extent of daylight is outside our usual measure, the nights in the far north of Britain being clear and short, so that there is only a brief time between dusk and the dawn half-light. So, they say, if no clouds intervene the sun's brightness is visible all night, not setting or rising but simply transiting. To be sure, the flat extremities of the land, with their low shadows, project no darkness, and night never falls beneath the sky and stars.

The land is tolerant of crops, except the olive, vine and other fruit of warmer countries, and is prolific of cattle. The crops are quick to sprout but ripen slowly, for a like reason, the plentiful moisture in the soil and atmosphere. Britain produces gold, silver and other metals, the prize of conquest. The sea produces pearls but somewhat cloudy and lead-coloured. Some judge their pearl-gatherers lacking in skill; for pearls are torn from the living breathing oyster in the Red Sea, while in Britain they are only collected when washed ashore: I can more readily believe that the pearls lack quality than that we lack greed.

SECTION 13: THE ROMAN CONQUEST

As for the Britons themselves, they freely discharge the levies, tributes and imperial obligations imposed on them, if there are no abuses; these they scarcely tolerate, submitting to domination, but not slavery. Julius Caesar, since deified, was the first of the Romans to invade Britain, overawing the natives in a successful campaign and making himself master of the coast (54BC), though he is seen rather to have revealed the island to posterity, than delivered it to them. Soon the Civil War was upon us; Rome's leaders turned their weapons on the State; and even though peace came Britain was long neglected. Augustus, since deified, called it policy, Tiberius precedent.

It is common knowledge that Caligula considered invading Britain (40AD), but his fickle mind was quick to repent of it, besides his great designs in Germany were frustrated. Claudius, since deified, took on the great task: legions and auxiliaries were shipped across (43AD), and Vespasian was there to play a part, the first of the distinctions that later came his way: tribes were conquered, chieftains captured, and Vespasian was revealed by destiny.

'The Emperor Claudius'
Laurens Eillarts, Antonio Tempesta, 1616 – 1620
The Rijksmuseum

Section 14: The first Consular Governors of Britain

The first consular governor appointed was Aulus Platius (43-47AD), soon followed by Ostorius Scapula (47-52AD), both distinguished military men; and the nearest regions of Britain were gradually enhanced to the condition of a province; a colony of veterans being founded also. Certain areas were handed over to King Cogidubnus (he has remained loyal down to our own times) according to the old and long-accepted custom of the Roman people, which even employs kings as useful tools.

Didius Gallus (52-57AD) who followed, maintained his predecessors' territory, and established a few forts in remoter areas, to gain credit for expanding the province. Veranius (57-58AD), who died within a year, succeeded Didius. After him, Suetonius Paulinus (58-62AD) experienced two years of success, subduing tribes and strengthening garrisons: and based on that success advanced towards the island of Mona (Anglesey) which harboured rebel forces, leaving his rear-guard exposed to surprise attack.

Section 15: Stirrings of Rebellion

With the governor absent, and their fears banished, the Britons began to discuss the ills of servitude amongst themselves, comparing their injuries, and accentuating their grievances: they argued that nothing was achieved by submission, other than that greater demands were placed on the willing sufferers. Once they each had one master: now two were imposed on them – a governor to extract their blood, a procurator their possessions. Whether working in harmony or discord the pair proved equally inimical to their subjects; one through his centurions, the other through his agents dealt violence and insults alike. Nothing was beyond reach of their greed or lust.

On the battlefield the stronger force plundered its enemy, but now it was mainly unwarlike cowards who raided their homes, abducted their children, and demanded levies, as though they would face death except for their country. How great, in fact, was this invading force, if the Britons were to count their numbers? Thus the Germans had cast off their yoke, with only a river and not an ocean to defend them. The Britons had their country, wives, parents to fight for; the enemy fought only out of greed and a desire for luxurious living; they would retreat, as their god Julius Caesar had retreated, if Britons would emulate the courage of their forefathers. Nor should they be cowed by the outcome of one or two battles: the successful may cut more dash, but greater persistence favours the underdog. Now the gods themselves were taking pity on the Britons, with the Roman governor distant, and his army relegated to a little island; and now they themselves had taken the most difficult step, that of opening the question to debate. Moreover in such matters the danger was not in being bold but in being discovered.

Section 16: Boudicca's Uprising and its Aftermath

Fired by such arguments as these, the whole nation took up arms, under the leadership of Boudicca (Boedicea), a woman of royal blood (since they recognise no distinction of gender among their rulers). After attacking the troops sparsely distributed among the Roman forts, and overcoming the garrisons, they invaded the colony itself (Colchester, 60/61AD), as the seat of oppression; no variant of barbarous savagery was omitted in their victorious rage. Had Suetonius Paulinus not learned of the uprising in his province and rushed to the rescue, Britain would have been lost. The outcome of a single battle restored its former submission; though the majority remained under arms, conscious of their failure, and in personal terror of the governor, fearing that despite his virtues he might deal ruthlessly with those who surrendered, punishing them severely as one who never overlooked an injury done to himself.

'Boudicca'

Character Sketches of Romance, Fiction and the Drama

Ebenezer Cobham Brewer (p270, 1892)

Internet Archive Book Images

Petronius Turpilianus was therefore appointed to the province (61AD), being less inflexible and new to any prior hostile actions, so more lenient if they repented of them. He settled their differences, but without attempting anything further, handing over to Trebellius Maximus (63AD). Trebellius, less energetic and with no military experience, held the province with a light touch, and even the barbarians learned to forgive the occasional moral error, while the interruption to civil strife provided a valid excuse for his inaction. But when the army, accustomed to fighting, became riotous in their idleness, there was trouble and discord. Trebellius, eluding the violence, by fleeing into hiding, shamed and humiliated, was then allowed to govern only on sufferance. There was a pact so to speak, that gave licence to the army, security to the governor, and an end to the mutiny, without bloodshed.

Nor did Vettius Bolanus (69AD) trouble Britain with discipline, during the strife in Rome; there was the same military inertia, the same disturbances in camp, though Bolanus, who was blameless and had done nothing to earn hatred, won the affection if not obedience of the men.

SECTION 17: CERIALIS APPOINTED BY VESPASIAN

However, once Vespasian had strengthened the empire, including Britain, with good generals and excellent troops the enemy hopes withered. Petilius Cerialis (71AD) instilled terror by invading the realms of the Brigantes, claimed as the largest tribe of the whole province: many battles were fought, some with great bloodshed; and by forays or extensive victories he annexed a large section of the tribe.

Indeed, Cerialis might well have eclipsed the efforts and fame of any other successor but Julius Frontinus, a great man, insofar as that was permitted, who accepted and sustained the burden, subduing by military force the powerful and warlike tribe of the Silures; overcoming the daring of the enemy, as well as the difficulties of the terrain.

SECTION 18: AGRICOLA'S ARRIVAL

Such was the state of Britain, such the military situation which Agricola found in the midsummer of his arrival when the troops, assuming campaigning was over, were seeking rest, and the enemy were seeking an opportunity. Shortly before his arrival, the Ordovices (of North Wales) had almost destroyed one wing of the army, and this initiative had roused the province. Those who desired war approved the action, and were waiting to see the reaction of their new governor.

Agricola, meanwhile, decided to confront the danger, although summer was now ending, his forces were scattered throughout the province, and his soldiers had ceased their campaigns for that year, which would hinder and delay a re-commencement, and despite the majority view which was rather for keeping an eye on the disaffected areas. He concentrated detachments of several legions, plus a small force of auxiliaries, and when the Ordovices refused to venture from the hills, directed the army to them, leading his men, to inspire others to face danger with equal courage. He almost eliminated the whole tribe, and aware of the need to follow up his success after that first campaign, in order to terrorise the rest, he determined to reduce the island of Mona (Anglesey), from whose conquest Paulinus had been recalled by the wider rebellion in Britain.

Not having anticipated the action, Agricola lacked the presence of the fleet: yet through his resourcefulness and determination the straits were bridged. Unloading the baggage train, he selected auxiliaries who knew the shallows, and had the skill in crossing at low tide attributed to their people, maintaining equal control of their own movements, their weapons and the horses; then he launched them suddenly, so as to astonish an enemy who expected ships, a fleet, by sea, and who concluded that nothing seemed difficult or proved impossible to those who waged war in such a way. So they sought peace, and surrendered the island, regarding Agricola as a great man, a brilliant general, who on entering the province, at the moment others spent in ostentation, courting attention, chose effort and danger. Even now, with success, Agricola refrained from boastfulness and talk of campaigns or victories, in controlling a conquered nation; nor did he attach laurels to his despatches; yet his deprecation of his achievements, added to them, considering how great his future hopes must have been given his silence regarding so great an outcome.

'A Map of Wales According to Ptolemy's Geography Rectified'

The History of Great Britain: From the First Invasion of it by the Romans

Under Julius Cæsar

Robert Henry, Malcolm Laing, John Adams (p531, 1789)

The British Library

SECTION 19: SOUND GOVERNANCE

Be that as it may, he was aware of the attitude of the provincials and, learning from others experience that force achieved little if injustice followed, he decided to eliminate the reasons for conflict. Beginning with himself and his entourage, he set his own house in order, which is as difficult a thing for most as to rule a province. He conducted no public business through slaves or even freedmen, admitting no soldier or officer to his staff through personal affection, or recommendation, or entreaty: but only the best of those he considered most loyal. Knowing everything, but not pursuing everything, he showed indulgence to small sins, severity towards the greatest, content often with a show of penitence, rather than forever exacting punishment; advancing to office and position those unlikely to offend rather than condemning those who did.

He mitigated the demands for grain and other tributes by equalising the burden, curtailing such schemes for profit as were harder to tolerate than the tribute itself. For example the game had been to force the natives to visit locked granaries, and buy grain to be left inside yet pay the price; or difficult roads and distant districts were nominated, so that tribes wintering nearby were forced to deliver in far off and out of the way places, until what should have been local to all produced profit for a few.

SECTION 20: IRON HAND, VELVET GLOVE

By immediately suppressing such evils in his first year, he gave a brilliant lustre to peacetime, which the indifference or arrogance of previous governors had rendered no less dreadful than war. Yet when summer came, he led his concentrated forces on many a campaign, commending discipline, coercing stragglers: he himself chose the sites for camp, he was the first to explore the estuaries and forests; and meanwhile no rest was allowed the enemy, who were no less prevented from sudden raids. Yet when he had sufficiently overawed them, by sparing them he again revealed the attractions of peace. In this way, many of the tribes that had remained independent were induced to grant hostages and abandon hostilities, and were then so skilfully and carefully surrounded by forts with Roman garrisons that never before had newly subdued areas passed to Rome with so little interference.

SECTION 21: CIVILISATION

The following winter was spent in prosecuting sound measures. So that a scattered and uneducated population, always ready on that account for war, might become accustomed through amenity to a quiet and peaceful life, he exhorted individuals and encouraged tribes to construct housing, market-places, and temples; praising the prompt, rebuking the idle, such that rivalry for compliments replaced coercion. Moreover he began to educate the chieftains' sons in the liberal arts, preferring native British intellect to any training obtained in Gaul, so that a nation which previously rejected the use of Latin began to aspire to eloquence therein. Furthermore the wearing of our clothing was seen as a distinction, and the toga became fashionable. Gradually they succumbed to the allurements of promenading, bathing, and fine dining. Inexperienced as they were, they called these aspects of their subjugation, civilisation.

SECTION 22: CAMPAIGNING IN THE NORTH

His third year of campaigning (79AD) uncovered new tribes, harrying them as far as Taus, as the estuary is named (Firth of Tay?). Filled with terror, the enemy did not dare to attack our forces, though these suffered from the atrocious weather, and there was the opportunity to establish forts. Those with experience noted that no general was more knowledgeable in their placement: no fort founded by Agricola was stormed by the enemy, or abandoned through capitulation and flight. There were frequent sallies, and the commanders were provisioned with a year's supplies against a lengthy siege. They faced the winter with intrepidity, each well secured, while the enemy were ineffectual and despairing, having been accustomed to set winter's gains against summer's losses, but now being driven off winter and summer alike.

Now Agricola was never desirous of taking credit for others' achievements: captain or colonel found him an honest witness to their feats. Some said he was more than severe in censure: though as gracious to the deserving as he was caustic to the undeserving. Nevertheless, his anger left nothing concealed, and there was no reason to fear his silence: he considered it nobler to disconcert than to hate.

SECTION 23: SECURING THE TERRITORY

The fourth summer (80AD) was spent securing the rapid gain in territory; and if the army's strength and the ambitions of Rome had allowed, he would have drawn a line only at Britain's furthest boundaries. But since Clota (the Firth of Clyde) and Bodotria (the Firth of Forth) carry the tidal waters of opposing seas far inland, and are separated by a short tract of territory, this was then fortified by Roman garrisons, and the whole of the neighbouring area secured, pushing the enemy back into almost a separate island.

SECTION 24: CAMPAIGNING ON THE WEST COAST OF SCOTLAND

In the fifth year of campaigning (81AD) he crossed in his flagship, and reduced hitherto unknown tribes in a series of successful battles; manning with troops that part of Britain which faces Hibernia (*Ireland*) rather in hopes of further activity than from fear, for Ireland, sited between Britain and Spain and open to the Gallic Sea, could unite two of the most worthwhile provinces of our empire, to their mutual advantage.

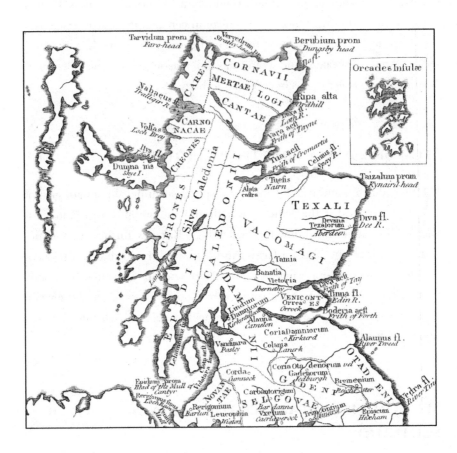

'A Map of Scotland According to Ptolemy's Geography Rectified'
The History of Great Britain: from the First Invasion of it by the Romans Under
Julius Cæsar – Robert Henry, Malcolm Laing, John Adams (p531, 1789)
The British Library

Ireland is smaller in size when compared to Britain, but larger than the islands of the Mediterranean. The soil, the climate and the character and manners of its inhabitants differ little from those of Britain, while its approaches and harbours are better known through trade and commerce.

Agricola had given sanctuary to a minor chieftain driven from home by faction, and held him, under the cloak of friendship, until occasion demanded. My father-in-law often said that with one legion and a contingent of auxiliaries Ireland could be conquered and held; and that it would be useful as regards Britain also, since Roman troops would be everywhere, and the prospect of independence would fade from view.

SECTION 25: CAMPAIGNING BEYOND THE FIRTH OF FORTH

Be that as it may, in the summer in which he began his sixth year of governance (83AD) he embraced the tribes beyond the Firth of Forth in his operations, fearing a general uprising among all the communities on that side, and he explored the coastline with his navy, nervous of land routes threatened by a hostile host. Agricola was the first governor to make the fleet an arm of his forces, a fine sight as it followed his progress, since the war was advanced by land and sea simultaneously. Often, soldiers, cavalrymen and marines shared their rations in mutual celebration, delighting in their various deeds and disasters, heights of mountain and forest on the one hand, trials of storm and sea on the other; comparing conquest of the foe and the terrain here, of the ocean there, in rival boast.

The Britons, equally, as captives related, were struck by the presence of the fleet: as though the hidden roads of the sea were laid bare, and the last sanctuary barred to the defeated. The Caledonian tribes resorted to armed warfare, appearing formidable, though more formidable in report, as is common with scarce known enemies. They made unprovoked attacks against the Roman forts, generating fear by their onslaughts. Cowards, advocating prudence, advised a retreat south of the Forth, ceding the territory rather than being expelled, in the midst of which Agricola learnt that the enemy were about to attack in force. Fearing to be surrounded, since the enemy was superior in numbers and their knowledge of the terrain, he split the army into three divisions and advanced.

SECTION 26: NIGHT ATTACK ON THE NINTH LEGION

Learning of this, the enemy quickly altered their plans, attacking the Ninth Legion, the weakest, in full force, killing the guards and breaking in to a scene midway between chaos and sleep. The battle was now within the camp itself, when Agricola, discovering the enemy line of march from his scouts and following in their footsteps, ordered the swiftest of his troops and cavalry to attack their rear-guard, and then raise a general cry, with dawn at hand, gleaming on the standards. The Britons were terrified, caught between two forces, as the Ninth regained their courage, and confident in their safety, fought for glory. They even sallied forth, and there was fierce fighting in the narrow gateway itself, until the enemy were repelled as the two Roman divisions fought to display, the one that they brought aid, the other that they had no need of rescue. Had the woods and marshes not saved the fugitives, that victory would have ended the campaign.

'Two Roman Soldiers'
Abraham Bloteling, 1652 – 1690
The Rijksmuseum

SECTION 27: THE BRITONS CONTINUE THE STRUGGLE

Fired by this knowledge, and given their reputation, the soldiers began to cry out that nothing could defy their courage or blunt their penetration of Caledonia, and that the furthest bounds of Britain must finally be secured in one unbroken campaign. Those who had been so prudent and cautious were now, after the event, eager and boastful. This is a most unjust aspect of war, that everyone claims victory for himself, and attributes defeat to one alone.

Equally, the Britons, considering themselves vanquished not in courage but by the general's timely strategy, were not a fraction less arrogant, but armed their young men, sent their women and children to places of safety, and ratified their confederacy by gathering to make sacrifice. So both sides separated in a state of excitement.

SECTION 28: MUTINY BY THE USIPII BATTALION

That same summer, a battalion of the Usipii, enrolled in Germany and shipped to Britain, committed a great and memorable crime. Murdering their centurions and the other soldiers, distributed among them as exemplars and instructors to instil discipline, they occupied three vessels, overcoming the helmsmen by force, one agreeing to join the oarsmen, the other two, being suspect, slain; and sailed past like a mirage before any rumour of it was known. Disembarking for water, and to forage for necessities, they fought with various groups of Britons who sought to defend their homes, and after frequent victories but finally defeat, they were reduced to such extreme starvation that they first ate the weakest of their company and then victims drawn by lot. In this manner they sailed round the coast of Britain, only to lose their ships on account of their lack of navigational skill. They were treated as pirates, and some were put to death by the Suebi, others later by the Frisii. Some were also sold as slaves, and so by a series of transactions reached our bank of the Rhine, the tale of their downfall rendering them notorious.

SECTION 29: LOSS OF HIS SON, AND ADVANCE TO MONS GRAUPIUS

At the beginning of summer (83AD), Agricola suffered the private blow of losing a son born to him the year before. He endured the event neither, as most strong men will, with bravado, nor with the mother's mourning and lamentation: but amidst the grief found relief in warfare. Thus he sent the fleet forward to descend on various places, and spread insecurity and terror; augmenting it with lightly-armed troops, strengthened by the most effective of the Britons, men proven during long years of peace, he advanced to Mons Graupius, which the enemy had occupied.

For the natives, still unbroken by the outcome of previous battles, with the prospect of Roman vengeance or slavery before them, aware by now that mutual danger must be repelled by common alliance, had summoned the tribes in strength, through envoy and treaty. Already in excess of thirty thousand men were in evidence, and still the warriors streamed in, those whose years were still fresh and green, noted in war, some wearing badges of honour, among whom the chieftain pre-eminent by courage and birth was named Calgacus. It is said he spoke in the following manner to the gathered host demanding battle:

SECTION 30: CALGACUS' SPEECH: 'THEY MAKE A DESERT...'

When I consider the causes of this war and our present situation, my spirit rises at the thought that this very day, and the unity you show, will bring freedom to all Britain; for united here and untouched by slavery, there is no land behind and the very sea is insecure, threatened as we are by the Roman fleet. So weapons and war, virtues to the strong, are also the best refuge of the coward. Previous battles, fought against Rome with varying success, leave the hope of salvation in our hands, for we the noblest of the Britons, dwelling in its furthest reaches, have never seen the shores of slavery, our eyes untouched by the stain of tyranny. To this day, on the last frontier of freedom, we have been protected by our very remoteness and obscurity; now the furthest shores of Britain lie exposed, and while the unknown is always magnified, now there are no more tribes, nothing but sea and stone, for these fatal Romans, whose arrogance you will not escape by humility and restraint. Thieves of the world, lacking lands now to devastate, they rove the sea. Those whom East nor West can satisfy reveal their greed if their enemies are wealthy, their ambition if they are paupers; alone amongst all men they covet rich and poor alike. Theft, slaughter, rapine they misname empire, they make a desert and call it peace.'

SECTION 31: CALGACUS' SPEECH: OF LIBERTY

Our children and kin are, by nature, the things most dear to us; they are carried off by levy to be slaves in other lands: our wives and sisters, even if they escape the soldiers' lust, are defiled by so called friends and guests. Our goods, our wealth are lost to tribute; our land and harvest to requisitions of grain; life and limb themselves in forging roads through marsh and forest, to the accompaniment of curses and blows. Slaves born to servitude are sold once and for all, and fed by their masters free of cost: Britain pays daily for her own enslavement, and daily nourishes it. And as among household slaves the newcomer is mocked by his fellows, so in this age-old worldwide house of slaves, we the newest and most worthless, are marked for destruction: we lack the fields, the mines, the harbours that we might have been preserved to labour in.

Pride and courage, moreover, in a subject displeases their rulers: our distance from them and obscurity, even as they protect us, make us more suspect. Therefore abandon all hope of pardon, and even now take thought, as to which is dearest, safety or glory. A woman led the Trinovantes to storm a camp and burn a colony, and if success had not lapsed to inactivity, they might have thrown off the yoke: let us, whole and indomitable, brought forth in freedom not regret, show at the first encounter, what manner of men Caledonia has chosen for her cause.'

Section 32: Calgacus' Speech: of Rebellion

'Think you the Romans, then, are as brave in war as they are lascivious in peace? Our discords and dissensions bring them success, their enemy's errors bring their armies glory. Those armies,

recruited from diverse nations, success holds together, defeat will dissolve. Unless you imagine that Gauls and Germans, and even, to their shame, many Britons, who lend themselves to an alien tyranny, its enemies longer than they have been its slaves, are swayed by loyalty and affection. Fear and terror are sorry bonds of love: remove them, and those who cease to fear will begin to hate. Every spur to success is ours: the Romans have no wives here to inspire them, no parents to reproach the deserter, and most have no other than an alien homeland. Few in numbers; fearful in their ignorance; the very sea, sky and forest, all they see around them, unfamiliar to their eyes, the gods have delivered them into our hands like prisoners in a cage. Empty show, the gleam of gold and silver, cannot terrify, that neither protects nor wounds. We shall find helping hands in the enemy's own battle lines. The Britons will acknowledge our cause is theirs, the Gauls will remember their former freedom: as the Usipii recently deserted them, so will the rest of the Germans. There is nothing beyond them to fear; empty forts, veterans' colonies, weak and quarrelsome townships of disaffected founders and unjust rulers. Here is leadership, and an army: there lies tribute, toil in the mines, and all the other ills of servitude, that you can perpetuate for ever, or avenge now, upon this field. Think then of your forefathers, and of your posterity, before you enter into battle.'

SECTION 33: AGRICOLA'S SPEECH: NO RETREAT

His speech they received with excitement, in the way barbarians will, with shouting, chanting and raucous cries. Then the armies formed ranks, weapons gleaming, the bravest to the fore. As the battle lines were drawn, Agricola, aware that his men, though full of spirit and hard to hold back behind their defences, needed further encouragement, spoke as follows:

'My fellow-soldiers, with the power and auspices of our Roman Empire backing you, and by loyalty and hard work, you have conquered Britain. Throughout these campaigns, on every battlefield, whether fortitude against our enemies or patience and effort against nature itself was needed, I have never regretted my faith in you, nor you in your leader. Thus I have exceeded the governors before me, and you the armies who preceded you; we mark Britain's bounds not by rumour and report, but with fortresses and arms: Britain is known, and conquered.

Often, on the march, when you were weary of rivers, mountains, marshes, I heard the bravest cry: "When will we see this enemy, test their courage?" They are here, dragged from their lairs; your prayers and effort are rewarded, all is with the victors and against the vanquished. It is honour and glory, now, to have marched so far, pierced forests, crossed estuaries, still advancing; but our prosperity of today makes for greater danger in retreat; we lack their knowledge of the terrain, their abundant supplies, but we have our sword-arms and in them we possess everything. As for me, I long ago determined that there is no safety in retreat for an army or its general. Therefore rather an honourable death than shameful life, and situated as we are safety and glory are one; nor would it be inglorious to die where earth and nature end.'

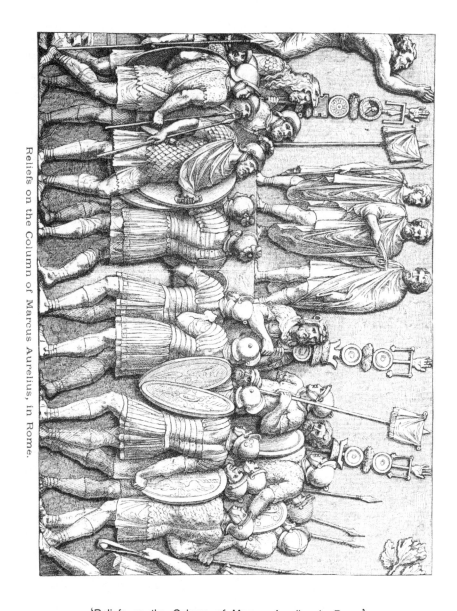

Reliefs on the Column of Marcus Aurelius, in Rome.

'Reliefs on the Column of Marcus Aurelius in Rome'
A History of all Nations from the Earliest Times
John Henry Wright (p225, 1905)
Internet Archive Book Images

SECTION 34: AGRICOLA'S SPEECH: COMPLETE THE WORK

'If fresh tribes and unknown forces confronted you, I would exhort you with the examples of other armies: as it is, simply recall your own efforts, use your own eyes. These are they who, furtively at night, attacked and were driven off by the noise of a single legion. These are they who of all the tribes of Britain fled the farthest, and thereby have held out the longest. When you penetrate the woodland glades, the creatures that are bravest charge at you, the timid and placid are driven off by the mere sound of your passing. So the fiercest of the Britons have already fallen, only a collection of timorous cowards remain. It is not because they made a stand that you have come upon them, but because they have been surprised. Your latest actions and their extreme fear have frozen their army in its tracks, so you may win a fine and glorious victory. Be done with campaigning, crown fifty years with one great day: prove to the Roman people that the army is not to blame for the war's delay or the rebels' chances.'

SECTION 35: THE DISPOSITION OF THE TROOPS

His troops' ardour was evident, even while Agricola was still speaking, and his oration ended in wild excitement, as they swiftly formed ranks. He placed his inspired and eager troops so that the auxiliary foot-soldiers, eight thousand strong, formed a powerful centre, with three thousand cavalry on the wings. The legions fronted the rampart, a source of great pride in the event of victory without shedding Roman blood, as reinforcements if the army was repulsed.

The Caledonian forces, so as to be at once impressive and alarming, were drawn up on high ground with the front ranks on the level and the rest seeming to rise higher and higher on the gentle slope; while the war-chariots filled the centre of the plain.

Then Agricola, fearing the enemy numbers were superior, extended his lines so as not to be attacked in front and on the flanks simultaneously, though his ranks would be stretched, and many called on him to deploy the legionaries, but he, more resolutely hopeful and firmly opposed to it, instead dismissed his mount and placed himself before the troops.

SECTION 36: ROMAN INFANTRY AND CAVALRY ATTACKS

The battle began with long range conflict; the Britons evading, or with their long swords and short shields brushing aside, our missiles, while on their part they launched great flights of spears. Eventually Agricola ordered four battalions of Batavi and two of Tungri to engage at sword-point, and hand to hand. This was an age-old tactic of theirs, difficult for the enemy to counter, their shields being too small to lock together, and their untipped long-swords too unwieldy for close fighting. Thus when the Batavi, exchanging blows, striking with their shield-bosses, stabbing at the enemy faces and, felling those who held the level ground, began to force their way uphill, the other battalions positioned themselves to charge in emulation, and slaughter those nearest, and in victory left many behind, lightly-wounded or even untouched.

Meanwhile, since the chariots had fled, our cavalry joined the infantry-battle. But though they caused momentary terror, they were stalled by the dense ranks of foes, and the sloping ground. It soon bore little resemblance to a cavalry action, as our troops, who had difficulty staying on their feet, were driven forward by the mass of horses; while the odd driverless chariot, its team panic-stricken, driven wild with terror, made oblique or head-on charges.

SECTION 37: ROUT OF THE CALEDONIANS

Meanwhile, the Caledonians, on the hill-tops not yet reached by the fighting, free to deride the smallness of our force, began to descend gradually and might have surrounded the rear of their attackers had not Agricola, fearing this, thrown four squadrons of cavalry, held in reserve, in their path, by whom the enemy were put to flight with a ferocity as great as the bravado of their assault.

So the Caledonians' tactic recoiled on themselves, since, at an order from our general, the front line squadrons switched to attacking the enemy from behind. Then began a great and bloody spectacle, wherever there was open ground: of pursuit, injury and capture, and as other fugitives crossed their path, slaughter of the captives. Now, the enemy, according to their nature, fled in armed groups before smaller numbers, or charged, though unarmed, of their own volition, and offered up their lives. Everywhere the field was covered with weapons, corpses, severed limbs and blood; but there was sometimes an angry courage even in defeat. For, as the Caledonians reached the woods, knowing the ground, they rallied and began to surround the foremost of their incautious pursuers. Had not Agricola ranged everywhere and ordered his strong, lightly-armed battalions to beat the woods, in the manner of huntsmen, along with cavalry, mounted where the woods were less dense, dismounted where they were thicker, over-confidence might have caused untold damage.

Be that as it may, the enemy, seeing the pursuit renewed by unbroken ranks of our troops,

turned to flight, not in groups as before, nor with any regard one for another, but scattering and taking evasive action made singly for their distant lairs. Night and a surfeit of conflict ended the pursuit.

There were ten thousand enemy dead: on our side three hundred and sixty fell, among them Aulus Atticus, a battalion commander, whose youthful ardour and spirited steed had carried him among the enemy lines.

'Ancient Roman Warriors Riding into Battle'

Antoine Caron (French, 1521 – 1599)

National Gallery of Art / NGA Images

SECTION 38: AFTERMATH OF VICTORY

A joyful night indeed of triumph and plunder for the victors: while the Caledonians dispersing, amidst the lamentations of men and women alike, dragged away their wounded, gathered those unhurt, and abandoned their dwellings, even setting fire to them in their anger. They found hiding places and as quickly eschewed them; now taking counsel together, now scattering; sometimes breaking down at the sight of their loved ones, more often stirred to action; it was credibly reported that some, as though in mercy, laid violent hands on wives and children. The following day revealed the extent of our victory more widely: all around was a silent waste, deserted hills, smoke rising from the ruined huts. Agricola's scouts, sent in all directions, met no one; the traces of the enemy's flight uncertain, and nowhere any sign of unity. And since warfare could not be conducted after the end of summer, he led his troops down to the territory of the Boresti. He took hostages from them, and ordered his naval commander to circumnavigate Britain. He granted him forces for the voyage, and terror ran before them. He himself, travelling slowly, so that the very leisureliness of his passage might strike fear into fresh tribes, reached winter quarters. Simultaneously the fleet, favoured by the weather and its reputation, gained the harbour of Trucculum, from which it had previously returned intact after coasting along the adjacent British shoreline.

SECTION 39: DOMITIAN'S REACTION

Domitian greeted this series of events, though Agricola's despatches were free of boastful language, with inner disquiet despite, as was his way, showing visible pleasure: he was conscious of the derision that his recent false triumph (83AD), celebrated over the Germans, had met with: for which in truth he had rented in the market-place a crowd whose clothes and hair simulated those of captives.

'Emporer Domitian'

Aegidius Sadeler, Marcus Christoph Sadeler, 1597 – 1629

The Rijksmuseum

Now here, a real and notable victory, with thousands of enemies slain, was being celebrated to great acclaim. That the name of a private individual should be exalted above that of the Leader, was what he most feared: it was useless to silence the forum's eloquence, and the noble arts of peace, if another were to grasp military glory. Moreover, while it was easy to ignore other qualities, those of leadership were an Imperial matter. Troubled by these anxieties, but content to keep them secret, a sign of his murderous intent, he decided to conceal his hatred for the time, until the first glow of fame and the army's plaudits had abated: since Agricola still held Britain.

SECTION 40: RETURN TO ROME

Accordingly, Domitian directed that whatever substituted for a triumph, including triumphal decorations, and the distinction of a public statue, should be accorded Agricola by a Senate vote, and enhanced by many fine phrases: and that a hint should be added that the province of Syria was destined for him, the governorship having been left vacant by the death of Atilius Rufus, of consular rank, and being reserved for mature candidates.

It was widely believed that a freedman of the inner circle was sent to Agricola with despatches in which Syria was granted him, having been instructed to deliver them only if Agricola remained in Britain; and that the freedman finding Agricola already this side the Channel, returned to Domitian without doing so, which may be true, or may be a fiction suggested by Domitian's devious ways.

'Roman Triumph'

Andrea Mantegna, 1486 – 1492

The Rijksmuseum

In the meantime, Agricola, having handed over a pacified and secure province to his successor, arrived in Rome (85AD) by night, so as to avoid public notice and a noisy reception, and evading his friends' welcome went that night to the palace as requested. Receiving a brief embrace, and not a word of enquiry, he melted into the crowd of courtiers. For the rest, to temper his military fame, offensive to the idle, with other virtues, he drank deep of the cup of leisure and tranquillity, modest in his dress, easy in conversation, attended by only one or two friends; so that society, whose habit it is to judge great men by their ostentation, seeing and noting Agricola, questioned the extent of his reputation, comprehended by few.

SECTION 41: AVOIDING THE LIMELIGHT

He was often denounced, in his absence, to Domitian during that time and, in his absence, acquitted. No crime was responsible for his predicament, no complaint by any victim of an offence; simply an Emperor hostile to virtue, the man's achievements and, worst of enemies, those who praise. Indeed a period of national troubles followed, in which Agricola should not have been ignored. Various armies in Moesia, Dacia, Germany and Pannonia were destroyed by the rashness or inattention of their generals (84-94AD) many battalions and their officers, were defeated and taken captive. Not only was the frontier of empire, the shore of the Danube, in danger, but the winter-quarters of the legions and the retention of whole provinces. So as the losses mounted, and every year witnessed death and disaster, popular voices began to demand Agricola's recall. His energy, stamina, and experience in war, was compared everywhere to the inertia and timorousness of the current military hierarchy. Of which mutterings sufficient reached Domitian's ears also; with his freedmen seeking, the best out of love and loyalty, the worst out of malice and jealousy, to influence a leader inclined to prefer the inferior. So Agricola was pushed precipitously towards the very attention he had avoided, both by his own qualities and others faults.

SECTION 42: AGRICOLA DECLINES A PROVINCE

The year arrived, in which lots were to be drawn for the governorship of Africa, and that of Asia Minor, whose previous governor, Civica, had recently been executed (in 88AD?), such that Agricola's caution was no less in evidence than Domitian's quiet menace. He was approached by certain of those aware of the Leader's intentions, who were to inquire, as if of their own accord, as to whether Agricola would accept a province. At first subtly praising peace and retirement, they were soon offering their own aid in support of his excusing himself from office, and finally, without further ado, advising and warning him, dragged him before Domitian. The Emperor, ready with his usual dissimulation, assumed a calm demeanour, listened to Agricola's request to be excused, nodded in approval, and allowed himself to be thanked, unashamed of granting such a plea out of envy. However he failed to gift Agricola a governor's usual salary, conceded by himself on occasion, offended by it not being sought, or out of conscience, not wishing it to appear as if the outcome had been bought. It is characteristic of human nature to hate those you have harmed: but in truth Domitian, though irritable by nature, and as unrelenting as he was secretive, was mollified by Agricola's moderation and discretion, who neither invited infamy and ruin through defiance or a foolish show of independence. Let those whose way it is to admire only what is rebellious, learn that great men can exist even under bad leaders, and obedience and moderation, if accompanied by industry and vigour, achieve that glory more often realised through dangerous actions, without benefit to the state, and an ostentatious end.

'Funeral of a Roman General'

Romeyn de Hooghe, 1672

The Rijksmuseum

SECTION 43: LAST ILLNESS AND DEATH

His final illness brought grief to us, sadness to his friends, and many an unknown stranger expressed concern. The general public, in this otherwise preoccupied city, came often to his door, and talked of him in the market squares and in private circles. No one who heard of his death was gratified or quick to forget him. Adding to the sorrow was a persistent rumour that he had been eliminated by poisoning: I would not venture to claim there is any evidence. However, during Agricola's illness, with a frequency unusual in a prince who appears by proxy, his leading freedmen and private physicians visited him, whether out of concern or policy.

When the final moment neared, every last breath was communicated to the palace by lines of messengers, none believing it would thus hasten any show of grief in Domitian. Yet he did show a kind of sadness in his manner and expression, his hatred tempered by feelings of renewed security, though he always concealed delight more easily than fear. It was evident that when Agricola's will was read, naming Domitian alongside the best of wives and the most dutiful of daughters, Domitian was delighted at the tactful offering. His mind was so blinded and corrupted by endless adulation he failed to see that good husbands and fathers make only bad princes their heirs.

SECTION 44: AGRICOLA THE MAN

Agricola was born on the 13th of June, in the third of Caligula's consulships (AD40) and died in his fifty-fourth year on the 23rd of August, in the consulship of Collega and Priscinus (AD93).

If posterity wishes to know of his outward appearance, he was more handsome than imposing: there was no aggressiveness in his look: his dominant expression was benign. You would easily have believed him to be a good man, and been glad to think him great. As for the man himself, though snatched away in his prime, he lived a long life if measured by his renown. He achieved those true blessings which reside in virtue; and what more could fortune have granted a man who had been a consul, also, and worn the ornaments of triumph?

He could not boast of excessive riches, but had ample wealth. With his wife and daughter surviving him, he might even pass for fortunate in escaping what was to come, his reputation unimpaired, in the flower of his fame, his friends and family secure. For though he did not live to see the light of this most fortunate age, with Trajan as our leader, which he foretold with prophecy and prayer in our hearing, nevertheless he was compensated, by a premature death, in evading those final days when Domitian, no longer fitfully or with pause for breath but in one single unremitting stroke, exhausted the life-blood of the state.

SECTION 45: AGRICOLA'S TIMELY END

He did not live to witness the Senate encircled by armed men, the House besieged, a host of men of consular rank slaughtered, in that same reign of terror, the flight and exile of so many noble women. Mettius Carus, the informer, had as yet only one success to his name; Messalinus' rasping voice of accusation was still confined to the Alban citadel; and Baebius Massa, that rascal, was still as yet on trial: soon our hands would drag poor Helvidius to prison; we it was who suffered Mauricus' and Rusticus' reproachful gaze; we who were drenched in innocent Senecio's blood. Nero averted his eyes, at least, and did not witness the evils he ordered: but under Domitian the worst part of our suffering was to see and be seen, so that our sighs might be noted down, that pallid cheeks enough might be observed by that brutal crimson face, buttressed against all shame.

Happy indeed, you were, Agricola! Not only in the brilliance of your life, but even in your timeliness in dying. Those who witnessed your last words say you faced death firmly and willingly; as though, as far as it lay with you, you might confess your Emperor innocent.

But to me, and to my wife, his daughter, besides the bitterness of losing a father is added our grief at not sitting beside his sickbed, comforting him in dying, sating our need to gaze on him and embrace him. To be sure we had received his wishes, his last requests to enshrine deeply in our hearts. But this was our sadness, a blow to us, that through the circumstance of our long absence he was lost to us four years before its end. I doubt not that all tributes due to you, best of fathers, were more than rendered in your honour, by the fondest of wives at your bedside; yet too few still were the tears shed as you were buried, and something your eyes longed for as they last sought the light.

SECTION 46: A FINAL SALUTE

If there is a place for virtuous spirits; if, as the wise are pleased to say, great minds are not extinguished with the body, rest in peace, and recall us, your family, from childish longing and womanish lament to the contemplation of your virtues, which it is wrong to grieve or mourn. Let us rather offer admiration and praise, and if our nature allows it, imitate you: that is true respect, that is the duty of his nearest and dearest. This I would preach to wife and daughter, to so venerate the memory of husband and father as to contemplate his every word and action, and to cling to the form and feature of the mind rather than the body; not because I think bronze or marble likenesses should be suppressed, but that the face of a man and its semblance are both mortal and transient, while the form of the mind is eternal, and can only be captured and expressed not through the materials and artistry of another, but through one's own character alone.

Whatever we have loved in Agricola, whatever we have admired, remains, and will remain, in men's hearts, for all time, a glory to this world; for many a great name will sink to oblivion, as if unknown to fame, while Agricola, here recorded and bequeathed to posterity, shall endure.

GERMANIA

'Gothic Buckle'
The Arts and Crafts of Our Teutonic Forefathers
Gerard Baldwin Brown (p204, 1910)
Internet Archive Book Images

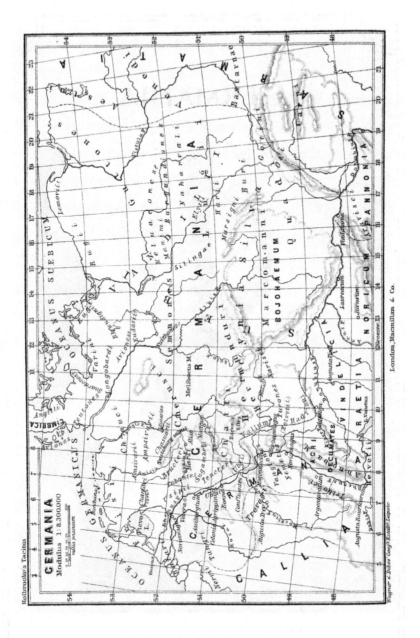

'Germania'

The Annals of Tacitus. Edited, with Notes, by G. O. Holbrooke

Cornelius Tacitus, George O. Holbrooke (p106, 1882)

The British Library

SECTION 1: THE LAND OF THE GERMANS

Germany, in its entirety, is separated from the Gauls, Raetians, and Pannonians by the Rhine and the Danube; and from the Sarmatians and Dacians by mountain ranges and mutual distrust: the remainder being bordered by the ocean, which washes broad peninsulas and islands of wide extent, various of whose peoples and leaders are only recently known to us, and whom warfare has revealed. The Rhine, rising from the precipitous and inaccessible heights of the Raetian Alps, after flowing in a slightly westerly direction, joins the North Sea. The Danube falling gently and gradually from the ridge of Mount Abnoba (*the heights of the Black Forest*) visits further peoples, until it flows, through six of its outlets, into the Black Sea: its seventh mouth being lost in the marshes.

SECTION 2: THEIR ORIGINS

As for the Germans themselves, I believe them to be indigenous and only minimally diluted through immigration by, or alliance with, other races, since those who have previously sought to change their homeland have arrived in ships and not by land, while the vast ocean beyond, and at the opposite end of the earth, so to speak, from us, is rarely visited by vessels from our world. Moreover, even ignoring the dangers of fearful unknown seas, who would leave Asia Minor, Africa or Italy to seek out Germany, a wild land with a harsh climate, dismal in aspect and culture unless it is one's own homeland?

Their traditional chants, the only kind of record or history they possess, celebrate a god, Tuisto, born of the earth. To him they assign a son Mannus, the origin of their race, and to him in turn three sons, the founders, from whose names the tribes nearest the ocean derive their appellation of Ingaevones, those in the centre that of Herminones, and the rest that of Istaevones. Some, with the licence due antiquity, declare the existence of further sons of the god, and additional tribal appellations, the Marsi, Gambrivii, Suebi, and Vandilii, and that these are the true and ancient names. Moreover, that the designation 'Germany' is a recent and late addition, and indeed the first tribes to cross the Rhine and drive out the Gauls, now called the Tungri, were then called Germans: the tribal name, while not yet the name of a nation, gradually increasing in usage, as they became known by the adopted name of 'Germans' first to their conquerors, on account of the apprehension roused, and later among themselves.

SECTION 3: HERCULES AND ULYSSES

They also claim that Hercules appeared amongst them, and on the eve of battle they sing of that bravest of all men. They also have a species of chant, they call *baritus*, the repetition of which inspires courage, and they divine the outcome of an imminent battle from the cry itself; they instil or show fear depending on the sound the warriors make, seeming to them not so much a concord of voices as of hearts. They principally affect a harshness of sound, a subdued roaring, their shields close to their mouths so that the voice echoing might achieve a fuller and deeper note.

To continue, Ulysses also, in the opinion of some authorities, during his long and fabulous wanderings was carried into this ocean, and reached the shores of Germany. Asciburgium (*Asberg*), sited on the banks of the Rhine and inhabited today, was founded and named by him; and also an altar dedicated by Ulysses, with the name of his father Laertes inscribed, was found in the same place, and tumuli and memorial stones carved with Greek letters are still extant in the borderlands between Germany and Raetia. I am not minded to confirm or refute these statements: each according to his opinion may diminish or augment their credibility.

SECTION 4: THE GERMAN PHYSIQUE AND NATURE

For myself I agree with the opinion of those who hold that the German peoples show no traits of intermarriage with other races, being individual, pure, like none other but themselves, such that all, so far as is known with regard to their extensive population, share a common physique: eyes which are fierce and blue in colour, reddish hair, and large frames unsuited to sustained effort: not being therefore tolerant of labouring and working hard, and little able to stand heat and thirst; but used to hunger and cold given their soil and climate.

SECTION 5: NATURAL RESOURCES

There are variations in the appearance of their terrain, but generally speaking it consists of either dense forest or unhealthy marsh, damper towards Gaul, windier towards Noricum and Pannonia: good for cereal crops, hostile to fruit trees, rich in livestock though the animals are, for the most part, undersized. The cattle are neither handsome nor possess majestic brows: boasting numbers only, but are the people's sole and welcome means of wealth.

E. M. Engelberts, inv. et delin.   H. Vinkeles sculp. 1785.

'Germanic Livestock and Agriculture'

Harmanus Vinkeles, 1785

The Rijksmuseum

The gods have them denied gold and silver, whether from mercy or in anger I cannot say (not that I would claim Germany devoid of gold or silver bearing veins, for who has explored it thoroughly?), though the people scarcely miss the possession or use of such metals. Silver vases may be seen there, gifted to their envoys and chieftains, but treated as of no more value than if they were made of clay; nevertheless the tribes closest to us treat gold and silver as precious metals for trade purposes, recognising and accepting certain coins of ours; though in the interior they simply barter goods in the primitive and ancient way. They prefer old and long-familiar coinage, for example the denarii with notched edges, stamped with a two-horse chariot. They rate silver more than gold, not because they are weak-minded, but because small silver coinage is more useful for common, low-cost purchases.

SECTION 6: WEAPONS AND WARFARE

Even iron is not abundant, as may be seen from their types of weaponry. Swords or the longer style of lance are rarely employed: they carry short spears, *frameae* in their vocabulary, with a short narrow blade, but so sharp and effective in use that they fight with the same weapon at close quarters or a distance, as circumstances demand. Their horsemen too are content with a shield and a *framea*: while the foot soldiers, naked or wearing only a light cloak, launch showers of the missiles, each hurling a volley over a wide space.

They boast no ornamentation, except that their shields are adorned with various colours. They own few breast-plates, while one or two at most have casques or helms. Their horses are noted neither for form nor speed; nor are they trained like ours to manoeuvre in a variety of directions: they are ridden straight forwards, or wheeling in a single movement to the right, turning together so that none are left behind. By common judgement more strength is accorded their foot-soldiers, and so all forces combine, with swift-footed warriors, skilled and apt for cavalry actions, being selected from the ranks of infantry. Their numbers are maintained at one hundred men from each canton: and that force labelled as such, 'the hundred', amongst them, so that what was once a mere number is now a badge of honour. Their armies are disposed in wedge formation. Yielding ground they consider a tactic and not evidence of cowardice, so long as one attacks again. They carry off their dead and wounded even in battles having an uncertain outcome. To abandon one's shield is the height of disgrace, men so shamed refused attendance at religious rites or council gatherings: many survivors of warfare end their shame with a noose.

'Germanic Troops'

Simon Frisius, 1616

The Rijksmuseum

SECTION 7: MILITARY STRUCTURE

They acknowledge chieftains on grounds of birth, but appoint their generals on grounds of courage, nor is a chieftain's power unlimited or exercised arbitrarily, while their generals lead rather by example than command, through admiration for their energy, and conspicuousness in the front rank. For the rest only their priests are allowed to inflict capital punishment, imprisonment, or flogging, and then not as a penalty on a general's orders, but as a command from the god whom they believe accompanies them to war. Certain effigies and emblems, brought from sacred groves, they carry into battle: but their greatest incitement to courage is that neither chance nor random association constitutes a squadron or a wedge, but rather family and kinship; and their partners are close by, so the woman's wail and the children's cries can be heard. These are the witnesses most precious to them, this is their greatest source of praise: to mothers, to wives they show their wounds, who do not shrink from demanding a sight of them, numbering the blows, and delivering food and encouragement.

SECTION 8: THE ROLE OF WOMEN

Their tradition tells that the uncertain and wavering ranks have sometimes been given new strength by the women's constant prayers, resolute front, and demonstration nearby that captivity, which they dread more on their women's account than their own, is at hand, so that a tribe's loyalty is more easily guaranteed when, with other hostages, a high-born daughter's presence is demanded.

Moreover they believe that women possess certain sacred and prophetic powers, so they are neither scornful of consulting them, nor neglectful of their answers. We know that, under Vespasian, Veleda was long-considered a deity by many; and they once revered Albruna too, and a host of others, and not merely out of flattery or as if they were about creating goddesses.

SECTION 9: WORSHIP OF MERCURY, MARS, ISIS AND HERCULES

They worship Mercury (*Wotan*) as greatest among the gods, he whom they hold it right to propitiate on certain days with human sacrifice. Hercules (*Donar*) and Mars (*Tiu*) they placate with whatever animal life is permissible. Some of the Suebi also sacrifice to Isis: though I have not discovered the source of, and reason for, this alien worship, only that its religious emblem, in the shape of a Liburnian galley, shows that the ritual was adopted from abroad.

'Germanic Offering'

Simon Frisius, 1616

The Rijksmuseum

They also judge, from the greatness of the divine, that a god should not be enclosed within walls, nor given the likeness of a human face, rather they consecrate woods and groves, and give sacred names to a mystery which only awe can behold.

SECTION 10: DIVINATION

They practise divination by lot, as readily as any people does: using a single method. A twig is cut from a nut-bearing tree, and split into slips: these are each uniquely marked, and then scattered randomly on a white sheet: next an official priest, on behalf of the people, or a patriarch in person, on behalf of his family, gazing at the sky and praying to the gods, selects three slips, one at a time, and interprets his choice according to the distinguishing marks they reveal: if the reading is negative, no further enquiry is made that day; if the reading is auspicious further confirmation by divination is sought. Though the Germans are also known to interpret the flight and calls of birds, their peculiar method is to consider the omens and premonitions arising from the behaviour of horses. Certain white ones are pastured at public expense amongst the woods and groves mentioned, and never harnessed for mundane human purposes; these they yoke to a sacred chariot bearing the priest, king or other chief of state, and they observe the horses' neighs and snorts. Not only the people, but their leaders, and priests place their greatest reliance on such divination; regarding themselves as servants, but the horses as messengers, of the gods.

They have one further method of divination, by which they foretell the outcome of major battles. A member of the tribe with whom they are at war is captured by one means or another, and pitted against a chosen champion of their own, each man wearing his tribe's armour. The victory of one or the other is taken as a presage of the wider result.

SECTION 11: THEIR METHOD OF GOVERNMENT

The chiefs resolve minor matters, the whole tribe major ones, but with this caveat, that even those matters which the people decide are first considered by their leaders. Unless there is some sudden emergency, they gather on particular days when the moon is new or at the full, believing those to be the most auspicious moments to initiate discussion. They reckon not by the days, as we do, but by the nights. So they appoint things, so they frame their agreements: the prior night being seen to determine the requisite day.

It is the fault of their love of liberty that they do not meet at once when commanded to do so, but two or three days may be wasted by their tardiness in assembling. Those gathered take their seats when it pleases them, fully armed. The priests, owning the right to insist, demand silence. Then chiefs or other leaders speak, according to seniority, status, military achievement, or eloquence, with authority to advise rather than power to command. If their suggestion displeases, it is rejected with groans; if it finds favour there is a clashing of spears: such expression of assent by martial acclaim is the most esteemed.

'Germanic Council Meeting'

Harmanus Vinkeles, 1786

The Rijksmuseum

SECTION 12: CRIME AND PUNISHMENT

Accusations may be made, and capital charges laid at this council meeting also. The death penalty varies with the offence. Deserters and traitors are hung from trees; cowards, objectors and deviants are drowned in muddy marshes under a wooden hurdle. The difference in method of execution reflects this: that certain crimes should be highlighted by the punishment, but the most shameful concealed. Lighter offences are punished accordingly: those convicted pay a fine of horses or cattle, part of which goes to the chief or the tribe, part to the victim or his relations. They also elect, among others, at these gatherings, the chiefs who will maintain the law through the villages and cantons, each man being assigned a hundred assistants from the people to act as his authorised advisors.

SECTION 13: RANK AND STATUS

They undertake no business, public or private, without being armed, though it is the custom that no man is allowed weapons until the community has approved his competence. His father, or relations, or one of the chiefs presents the young warrior with shield and spear: it is the equivalent of granting the toga, the first youthful honour. Prior to that he is seen as part of the household, afterwards a subject of the state. High birth, or great paternal merit, win distinction from the leadership, even for the very young. They mix with the stronger, more mature warriors, proven by previous service, and are not ashamed to be seen among their followers. Rank is indeed observed among such a retinue, which depends on the leader's favour, such that there is great rivalry among his comrades as to who shall be second only to the chief, and likewise among the chieftains as to which has the largest and bravest set of followers. This is status, this is power, to be always surrounded by a large select band of young men, an adornment in peace, a defence in war. It not only brings fame and glory to a warrior among his own people, that his retinue is known for its numbers and bravery, but also among neighbouring tribes; such men being requested as ambassadors, honoured with gifts, and often their very name is enough to resolve conflict.

SECTION 14: THEIR EAGERNESS FOR WARFARE

Once engaged in battle, it is shameful for a chieftain to be outdone in courage, shameful for his followers not to match the bravery of their leader. To desert the field and survive one's prince indeed means a lifetime of reproach: to defend and protect him, to devote one's deeds to his greater glory, is recognised in their primary oath of allegiance: the leader fights for victory, the followers for their leader.

If the tribe in which they are born is becalmed in a long period of peace and quiet, many noble youths, of their own will, seek tribes engaged in some war or other, because peace is unwelcome to their race, and it is easier to gain renown in troubled times. Moreover, a large retinue demands war and violence, since it is their prince's liberality that provides the mighty warhorse, the murderous all-conquering spear, the banquets and, though coarsely-wrought, the still lavish accoutrements that serve as their pay. The basis of such munificence is through war and rapine. You will find it harder to persuade them to till the land and await the harvest, than challenge the enemy and earn their wounds. On the contrary, it seems weak and shiftless to them to acquire by sweat what you can win with blood.

E. M. Engelberts, inv.   H. Vinkeles sculp. 1785.

'Germanic War Exercises'

Harmanus Vinkeles, 1785

The Rijksmuseum

SECTION 15: THEIR IDLENESS IN PEACE

Whenever they are not engaged in war, they spend much time in hunting, more in idleness, given to food and sleep, the strongest and bravest warriors doing nothing, delegating the care of hearth and home, as well as the cultivation of their fields, to the women, the aged, and the most infirm of their household. They themselves vegetate, through that strange paradox of nature by which the same individuals both love idleness and loathe peace.

It is a custom among the tribes for each man, freely, to grant some portion of his cattle or crops to his chieftain, which is received as an honour but also serves his needs. Their leaders value the gifts of neighbouring tribes even more highly, since they are offered by whole peoples not merely by individuals, for example choice steeds, magnificent armour, roundels and torques; while we have now accustomed them to accept coins also.

SECTION 16: HOUSING

It is well known that none of the German tribes are urbanised, homes among them not being allowed in close proximity. They live apart, scattered, as fountain, field and grove appeal to them. Their villages are not built after our fashion with buildings near together and connected, rather each man surrounds his house with a clear space, either as a precaution in case of fire, or through lack of expertise in construction. They use neither quarry-stones nor tiles, while the timber they employ for everything is uncarved, without ornament or decoration, though certain areas are coated carefully, and are bright and gleaming enough to substitute for paint and frescoes. They also excavate subterranean *fogous*, piling dirt on the roof, as a store and winter-shelter for produce, since such places mitigate the frost's rigour, and if enemies attack they will lay waste all above ground, but what is hidden below is either not known of, or escapes by its very nature, its discovery requiring a thorough search.

E. M. Engelberts, inv. et delin.   H. C. Vinkeles, sculp. 1784.

'Hunting, Fishing and Relaxation'

Harmanus Vinkeles, 1784

The Rijksmuseum

SECTION 17: CLOTHING

All wear a cloak for clothing, fastened with a brooch or, failing that, a thorn: and otherwise naked will spend whole days round the hearth and its fire. The richest are distinguished by undergarments, not loose like Parthians or Sarmatians, but tight and moulded to the limbs. They also wear the pelts of wild creatures, those tribes by the Rhine and Danube in casual mode, the remoter tribes giving them more attention, since such are not available from merchants. The hides are choice, and those selected are ornamented with the variegated pelts of sea-creatures from the far ocean and its unknown waters.

The women's clothing is similar to the men's, except that the women are often veiled in linen garments striped with purple, the upper part without sleeves so that the shoulders and arms are bare, and the adjoining portion of the breast is visible.

SECTION 18: MARRIAGE

However, the marriage laws are strictly observed among them, and you will find nothing more laudable in their customs. They, almost alone among barbarians, are content with a single wife: the very few exceptions being embraced not out of libidinous desire, but to strengthen the nobility by multiple ties.

'Two Germans'

Anonymous, 1614 – 1616

The Rijksmuseum

A dowry is not offered by the wife to the husband, but by the husband to the wife. The parents and relations gather round to approve the gifts, ones not designed to delight women or adorn the bride, but oxen, a horse and bridle, a shield, spear, or sword. The wife is received with these gifts, and she in turn offers some piece of weaponry to her husband. Thus marriage is sealed by an ultimate bond, a mysterious sacrament, by the gods themselves: lest the wife think herself absolved from considerations of bravery, and the fortunes of war, she is warned by the very rituals with which her marriage begins that she is to share effort and danger, to toil and venture together whether in peace or amongst conflict. This is what the yoked oxen, or bridled horse, or gift of arms denote. So must she live, so bear children: accepting what shall be handed on intact and honoured, to be received by her daughters-in-law, and passed down in turn.

SECTION 19: FEMALE CHASTITY

So the women exist, fenced-in and chaste, without seductive display, uncorrupted by the incitements of the dinner-table. The exchange of secret letters is unknown to male or female. Adultery by a married woman is infrequent considering the size of population, and its punishment is swift, being the husband's prerogative: the husband drives her, her head shaved and her body stripped naked, from his house, in front of the relatives, and whips her through the village; there is no pardon for publicly acknowledged loss of chastity: neither beauty, youth nor wealth will find her a husband. No one laughs at vice there, no one calls corrupting or being corrupted the nature of the times. Better still are the tribes where only virgins wed, and seal it once and for all with the vows and prayers of marriage. Thus they accept one husband only, so that, as one flesh and one being, without lingering thoughts or belated desires, they might love not simply the man, but marriage itself. To limit the number of their children, or do away with a later-born child is held as an abomination, while among them fine morals have more force than fine laws elsewhere.

SECTION 20: RAISING OF CHILDREN

Thus the children of every house flourish, despite nakedness and squalor, to acquire that size of body and limb at which we marvel. The mother suckles a child at her own breast, without wet-nurses and maids.

Master and servant are not distinguished by any niceties of upbringing: they live on the same earth-floor among the same cattle, until the years separate nobleman from commoner, and manhood claims them.

Sexuality comes late to young men, and puberty is not enfeebled; nor is girlhood forced; they are of similar stature, equals in age and maturity when they are mated, and the children reflect the parents' vigour. A sister's offspring are as honoured by her brother as by her husband. Some tribes hold this blood-tie as closer and more sacred than that between father and son, and give it the greater stress when taking hostages, as though they thereby grasp a house more comprehensively and its ruling spirit more securely.

Yet, each man's offspring are his heirs and successors, even without a will. If there are no children, the closest relatives to inherit are brothers, paternal uncles, then maternal uncles. The more relations a man has, and the greater the number of his connections by marriage, the more influential he is when old; there is no prize there for being without ties.

'Domestic Life'

Harmanus Vinkeles, 1784

The Rijksmuseum

SECTION 21: REPARATION AND HOSPITALITY

A father's or kinsman's enmities must be pursued, no less than his friendships, though such feuds do not remain unresolved for ever: even murder is appeased by a certain number of cattle and sheep, and a whole house receives satisfaction to everyone's advantage, since feuds are more dangerous when conjoined with freedom of action.

No people indulge more lavishly in feasting and hospitality. It is a crime to close the door to any human being. Everyone offers a well-appointed table, according to their wealth. When the time comes, he who has been your host, points out your next port of call, and accompanies you. You go to a nearby house, without invitation but that is no matter: you are received there with equal kindness. No one distinguishes between strangers or acquaintances where the laws of hospitality are concerned. It is usual to offer the parting guest anything he fancies: there is the same readiness to make requests in turn. They delight in the exchange of gifts, but neither take account of what they have given nor feel obliged to reciprocate what they have received. Manners between host and guest are always courteous.

SECTION 22: THEIR BANQUETS

W aking from sleep, which they usually extend into the daylight hours, they wash, generally in warm water, since winter dominates so much of their lives. Having washed, they take food: each seated apart at their own table. Then to business, or as often to enjoyment, weapon in hand. It is no reproach to spend day and night drinking. Quarrels are frequent, as usual among the inebriated, seldom ended merely with invective, more often with bloodshed and wounds. Yet reconciliation between enemies, the forming of family alliances, the appointment of leaders, even questions of peace or war, are commonly debated at these banquets, as though at no time are their minds more open to honest thought or more greatly inspired. A race without cunning or guile, in the liberty such gatherings allow they expose things previously hidden in the heart; so every thought is laid bare. The next day all is reviewed, and its rightness on each occasion justified: they deliberate when incapable of pretence, and decide when free from illusions.

SECTION 23: THEIR DIET

They drink distillations of wheat and barley, fermented to something resembling wine: the tribes nearest the Rhine and Danube buying wine itself. Their diet is simple, wild fruits, fresh game, and curdled milk: they satisfy their hunger without undue preparation or blandishment. But there is not the same moderation where drink is concerned. If you indulge their thirst by supplying what they crave, they will be conquered by that vice as easily as they are in battle.

SECTION 24: THEIR PASTIMES

Their pastimes are all of one kind, and the same whatever the gathering. Youths, for whom this is sport, leap and bound between swords and menacing spears. Practice makes them skilful and skill brings grace, but not for gain or reward: however bold the sport, their only prize is the spectators' pleasure. Gambling, surprisingly, they indulge in as a serious pastime while sober, so reckless in winning or losing, that when all else is gone, they will stake their own freedom on one further and final throw. The loser faces voluntary servitude: though the younger and stronger man, he allows himself to be bound and sold. To such an extent is their pig-headedness or, as they would term it, their honour involved in this wicked practice. Slaves, so created, they put up for sale, to absolve themselves also of the shame of such a victory.

'Germanic Banquet'

Philippus Velijn, 1825

The Rijksmuseum

SECTION 25: SLAVES AND FREEDMEN

Their other servants are not, as with us, given precise roles within a household: each rules his own house and home, while his master demands a certain amount of grain or clothing or a number of cattle from him, as if he were a crofter, and with this the servant complies. The rest, the household tasks, are performed by the master's wife and children. To beat a servant, or oppress him by hard labour or imprisonment, is rare: the death of a slave is not usually a matter of disciplinary severity but the result of a blow struck in anger, as against an enemy except that no penalty is incurred.

Freedmen are not much higher in status than slaves: rarely of much account in the household, and of none in public life, except among the predominant tribes, where they may rise above the free-born and even nobles. Elsewhere, the freedman's inequality attests to others freedom.

SECTION 26: LAND MANAGEMENT

To utilise capital and increase it by levying interest is unknown; and the avoidance of it is therefore more strict in the observance than if it were prohibited. The land is claimed, area by area, by whole communities according to their number of farmers, and then allocated among these on the basis of rank, the distribution facilitated by the wide tracts of country available. They change the fields under cultivation annually, and there is still land to spare. Nor do they task the soil's fertility and yield by planting orchards, setting apart water-meadows, or irrigating market gardens. Grain is their only harvest, so that the year is not split into as many agricultural seasons as ours: winter, spring and summer are acknowledged and so designated, but the name and the fruits of autumn are unknown.

SECTION 27: FUNERAL RITES

Their funerals are unostentatious: their only observance is to cremate the bodies of their prominent men on a pyre made of choice woods, but free of perfumes and palls: to each man is his armour, while for some the body of their charger helps fuel the flames. The tomb is a mound of turf: they reject the labour and difficulty of building a monument that would weigh too heavily on the dead. They soon cease weeping and lament; while sorrow and sadness linger. It is honourable for the women to mourn, while the men simply remember those gone.

All this we have established regarding the common origins and customs of the German people: I will now describe the customs and habits of the various tribes, in as much as they differ from one another, and explain which of them have migrated from Germany to the Gallic provinces.

'Germanic Funeral Rites'
Reinier Vinkeles, 1788 – 1790
The Rijksmuseum

SECTION 28: MIGRATIONS OF THE GERMANS AND GAULS

It is recorded, on the supreme authority of Julius Caesar, now worshipped as divine, that the Gauls were once more powerful than the Germans; and therefore it is credible that they crossed into Germany. There was little likelihood of the rivers preventing each tribe, as it grew in strength, from seizing the common land, not yet divided into mighty kingdoms, and occupying it in turn. So, the country between the Hyrcanian Forest and the rivers Rhine and Main was taken by the Helvetii, and that beyond by the Boii, both Gallic tribes. The name Bohemia is still in use, a historical witness to its ancient occupants, despite the changes.

It is however uncertain whether the Illyrian Aravisci migrated into Pannonia from the region of the Osi, or the Osi into Germany from that of the Aravisci, since their language, customs and manners remain the same, there being originally an equal degree of freedom and equal deprivation on either bank of the river, the same advantages and disadvantages.

Conversely the Treveri and Nervii are keen to claim a Germanic origin, as though this noble ancestry distances them from any affinity with the sluggish Gauls.

Along the banks of the Rhine itself live tribes that are indisputably German: Vangiones, Triboci, Nemetes. Not even the Ubii, though they have earned the right to form a Roman colony (*Cologne*), and prefer to be called Agrippinenses from their founder, are embarrassed by their origins, having previously crossed the river and, after proving their loyalty, been stationed on the banks of the Rhine, not so as to be under observation, but as a barrier to others.

SECTION 29: THE BATAVI AND MATTIACI

The bravest of all these tribes are the Batavi, scarce along the Rhine, but occupying an island fork in its stream. Once part of the Chatti, they crossed the river, due to domestic conflict, to a region that brought them into the Roman Empire. That distinction and the mark of ancient alliance persists; since they are not insulted by having to pay tribute, and are not oppressed by taxes. Exempted from the burden of contribution, singled out only for battle, they are reserved for war, like weapons and armour. The tribes of the Mattiaci, are part of the same system of alliances; for the greatness of the Roman people has inspired reverence beyond the Rhine, our former frontier. By location and boundaries they belong to the far bank, but in mind and spirit they act with us, similar to the Batavi in other respects except in so far as the climate and soil of their land of themselves induce in them greater animation.

I will not number those tribes who cultivate the 'ten cantons' among the German peoples, even though they have established themselves beyond the Rhine and Danube. All the most fickle of the Gauls, rendered audacious by deprivation, occupied that doubtful region; which is, now the frontier has been extended and the garrisons pushed forward, regarded as a corner of the Empire and part of a province (*Upper Germany*).

'The Coming of the Batavians'

Simon Fokke, 1725 – 1784

The Rijksmuseum

SECTION 30: THE CHATTI – MILITARY CAPABILITIES

B eyond, with the Hercynian uplands, begin the first settlements of the Chatti. Their land is not as level and marshy as that of the other territories comprising Germany; but though the hills are extensive they gradually thin out, and the Hercynian forest after embracing its Chatti finally deposits them in the plain. The tribe has a tougher physique, with tight-knit limbs and a threatening look, than the others, and greater mental vigour. They show a substantial degree of method and expertise, for Germans: they appoint men of their own choice, listen to those appointed, observe rank, perceive opportunities, delay their attacks, organise during daylight hours, retrench at night, distrust luck and depend on courage, and rarest thing of all, except where Roman discipline pertains, rely more on the commander than on his men.

Their whole strength is in their infantry, whom beside their weapons they weigh down with iron implements and baggage: other tribes seem prepared for a fight, the Chatti for a war. Forays and chance encounters are infrequent: the latter being a strength more of cavalry squadrons, suddenly winning ground and as suddenly retiring: while for infantry speed may become panic, just as caution is allied to steadiness.

KATTENWALD EN CESAR.

'Kattenwald, Leader of he Chatti, Shakes Hands with Julius Caesar'

Dirk Jurriaan Sluyter, 1826 – 1886

The Rijksmuseum

SECTION 31: THE CHATTI – MILITARY CUSTOMS

One practice, adopted by other German tribes only rarely, and by courageous individuals, is customary among the Chatti, namely for youths to let their hair and beard grow long on reaching manhood, and only rid themselves of what cloaks the face, and is vowed and pledged to courage, once they have killed an enemy combatant. They reveal their shorn aspect above the bloody spoils, and only then declare they have repaid the debt due their birth and are worthy of their kind and country: cowards and weaklings must remain unkempt. The bravest also wear an iron collar (a badge of shame among this people) as if fettered, until freed from it on killing an enemy: this custom is widely adopted among the Chatti, and men already grown grey are distinguished so by friends and enemies alike. Every battle is initiated by these warriors: they always form the front rank, a curious sight: and even in peacetime they submit to no tamer way of life. None has house or land or occupation: wherever they go they are feted, profligate of other's wealth, indifferent to possessing wealth themselves, until the debility of age renders them unequal to so harsh a display of virtue.

SECTION 32: THE USIPI AND TENCTERI

Closest neighbours to the Chatti are the Usipi and the Tencteri, along the Rhine where the river's course is fixed enough as to act as a frontier. The Tencteri, besides the customary fitness for war excel in the skilled disciplines of horsemanship; the fame of the Chatti's foot-soldiers not exceeding that of the Tencteri's cavalry. As their ancestors appointed, so their descendants follow in turn. In such practices lie the child's games, the rivalries of youth, and the lasting interest of old-age. Their horses are passed down along with the house, the servants, the rights of succession: but in the case of the horses not, as otherwise, to the first-born son, but to the one who is fiercest in war, and the finer warrior.

SECTION 33: THE BRUCTERI, CHAMAVI AND ANGRIVARII

The Bructeri used to live alongside the Tencteri: now the Chamavi and Angrivarii are said to have moved in, the Bructeri having been expelled, banished by a consensus of neighbouring tribes who hated their arrogance or were attracted by the delights of plunder, or because the gods favoured us Romans, not even begrudging us sight of the conflict. More than sixty thousand warriors fell, and not to our swords and spears, but more magnificently still simply to feast our eyes. I pray that it may last, long enduring among the nations though no source of love for us, this firm hatred of each other, since, the destiny of empire urging us on, Fortune can grant us nothing better than discord between our enemies.

SECTION 34: THE DULGUBNII, CHASUARII, AND FRISII

The Angrivarii and the Chamavi are bordered on the south by the Dulgubnii and the Chasuarii and other tribes as little known, while to the north are the Frisii, called Lesser and Greater according to their strength of numbers. These two tribes inhabit the Rhine down to the sea, and also border the large lakes that Roman fleets have navigated. We have even attempted the ocean waves themselves, and tradition suggests that there are equivalents to the Pillars of Hercules beyond, either because Hercules was actually there, or because we consent to the attribution of all such wonders to him. Germanicus was not short of daring, but the ocean denied him extensive inquiry regarding itself or Hercules. Further attempts were abandoned, it being thought more pious and reverential to believe in the works of the gods than to try and fathom them.

SECTION 35: THE CHAUCI

U p to this point we have been considering western Germany; now the land sweeps away in a vast northwards curve. The first tribe encountered is the Chauci, who though occupying a stretch of the seaboard also border on the tribes mentioned, and skirt south as far as the Chatti. This immense area of land is not merely held by the Chauci, but densely populated by them. They are the noblest of German tribes, choosing to defend their vast territory through the rule of law alone. Neither grasping nor violent, living in peace and quiet, they provoke no wars, nor do they raid and plunder their neighbours. The prime argument for their virtue and strength is this, that their superiority is not founded on injustice. Yet they are prompt with arms, and if circumstances demand them, armies, with a wealth of men and horses; maintaining that reputation in peacetime.

SECTION 36: THE CHERUSCI AND FOSI

B ordering the Chauci and Chatti are the Cherusci, who, undisturbed for many years, have nourished an excessive and enervating placidity: a delightful but unsafe policy, since peace bordered by power and lawlessness is illusory: where force acts, discipline and righteousness are titles given to the strongest. Thus, the Cherusci, once called just and generous, are now described as spineless fools, while the victorious Chatti's good fortune is ascribed to wisdom. The Cherusci's decline, dragged down the Fosi, their neighbours, who are now their equals in adversity, having been merely their inferiors in prosperous times.

'The Cherusci Commander Arminius Defying the Romans'

Reinier Vinkeles, 1751 – 1799

The Rijksmuseum

SECTION 37: THE CIMBRI

The Cimbri inhabit this same arm of Germany nearest the sea, a small tribe now but great in fame. Wide traces of their ancient glory remain, large encampments on both banks of the Rhine, by whose size you can gauge even today the strength and numbers of that people, witness to a vast exodus.

Rome was in its six hundred and fortieth year *(114/113BC)*, Caecilius Metellus and Papirius Carbo being consuls, when the Cimbrian forces were first heard of. Counting from that date to the time of Emperor Trajan's second consulship *(AD98)* is a space of about two hundred and ten years: so long has it taken to conquer Germany. Throughout that vast period there have in turn been many losses. The Samnites, the Carthaginians, Spain, Gaul, not even the Parthians have taught us more costly lessons: the German struggle for freedom has been fiercer than Arsaces' for Parthian dominance.

What taunt can the East deliver, other than Crassus' defeat *(53BC)*, having itself lost Pacorus, a prince falling at the feet of Ventidius *(38BC)*. While the Germans instead defeated or captured Carbo *(at Noreia, 113BC)* and Cassius Longinus *(Garonne Valley, 107BC)*, Servilius Caepio and Maximus Mallius *(Orange, 105BC)*, broke five of Rome's consular armies in one campaign, and even snatched Varus and three legions from Augustus Caesar. It was not with impunity that Marius struck them in Italy *(Raudine Plain, 101BC)*, the deified Julius in Gaul *(58-55BC)*, and Drusus, Tiberius and Germanicus on German soil *(12BC-AD16)*. Later Caligula's vast threats turned to farce. Then little, until taking advantage of our dissension and civil war *(AD69)* they stormed the legions' winter quarters, and even aimed at the Gallic countries. Finally repulsed, they have, in recent times, more often found defeat than victory.

SECTION 38: THE SUEBI

Now I must speak of the Suebi peoples, not merely a single tribe like the Chatti or Tencteri. They hold the greater part of Germany, and though generally called Suebi have also their individual tribal names. A mark of these peoples is to comb and tie their hair aslant into a dangling knot: this distinguishes the Suebi from other Germans, and the free-born Suebi from the slave. The same thing may be found in other tribes, either due to their relations with the Suebi, or from imitation, as so often happens, but it is rare and confined to youth. Among the Suebi, even till the hair turns grey, the coarse locks are twisted back, and often knotted on the crown of the head itself. The chieftains wear theirs ornamented, mindful of their appearance but in all innocence; not with a view to admiring or being admired, but being more fittingly adorned for enemy eyes, when facing battle, if they achieve a somewhat terrifying height.

SECTION 39: THE SEMNONES

They regard the Semnones as the most ancient and noblest of Suebi; the proof of their antiquity confirmed by religion. At certain times, in age-old reverence for their ancestral prophetic lore, all those of the same names and blood gather in delegations at the sacred grove, and publicly offer up a human life, as a dreadful beginning to their barbarous rites. And there is another respect they pay the grove: no one enters unless bound with rope: acknowledging by this their inferiority and the power of the deity. If they chance to stumble, they must not rise or be lifted: but crawl out over the ground: the whole superstition derives from this, that here the race arose, here dwells the god of all; all else obeys and is submissive. The Semnones' wealth adds to this authority: they possess a hundred cantons, a number whose size leads them to believe themselves the leaders of the Suebi.

SECTION 40: THE LANGOBARDI AND OTHERS

The Langobardi, on the other hand, are famous despite their lack of numbers: surrounded by numerous powerful tribes, they are rendered secure by a willingness to take risks and by conflict. Then there are the Reudigni, Aviones and Anglii, the Varini, Eudoses, Suarines and Nuitones, protected by rivers and forest. There is nothing notable about them individually, but they all worship Nerthus, or Mother Earth, and conceive her as intervening in human affairs, by riding among the peoples. For on an island in the sea lies a sacred grove, and in it a chariot covered with a robe, which a single priest is allowed to handle. It is he who detects the presence of the goddess in her sanctuary, following with reverence as she is drawn away in her chariot by heifers. Then there are days of rejoicing, in whichever festive places are worthy to receive and host her. They make no war, assume no arms, lock up their weapons, only then are peace and quiet known and loved, until she is sated with human society, and the priest returns her to her sanctuary. Then chariot, robe, and if you wish to believe so, the goddess herself are washed in a hidden pool: the slaves who minister to her being immediately swallowed by the waters. Hence arises a secret terror and a sacred mystery, as to what that might be that they witness only to die.

SECTION 41: THE HERMUNDURI

These tribes of the Suebi extend into more distant parts of Germany: nearer to us, if I now follow the Danube's course as a moment ago I followed the Rhine's, is the territory of the Hermunduri, allies of Rome; with them alone among the Germans we trade not only along the river but in the interior, and with the province of Raetia's most illustrious colony. The Hermunduri traverse the river unwatched, and while we only let others see our fortified encampments, we reveal our houses and homes to them, who are not covetous. Among the Hermunduri the River Albis (*Elbe*) rises, once familiar to us and famous, now little heard of.

SECTION 42: THE MARCOMANI, NARISTI AND QUADI

Close to the Hermunduri are the Naristi, then the Marcomani and Quadi. The fame and power of the Marcomani are pre-eminent: their very land itself was won by their former expulsion of the Boii. Nor are the Naristi or Quadi inferior. These tribes are, if you wish, Germany's brow, wreathed, so to speak, by the Danube. The Marcomani and the Quadi were ruled by kings of their own race down to our own times, the noble houses of Maroboduus and Tudrus (now they submit to foreign rulers), but the strength and power of such kings depends on Roman influence. On occasion we aid them with troops, more often with cash, which is no less valuable to them.

SECTION 43: THE MARSIGNI, LUIGI AND OTHERS

Beyond them are the Marsigni, Cotini, Osi and Buri, enclosing the Marcomani and Quadi on their rears. Of these the Marsigni and Buri recall the Suebi in language and culture: while the Cotini's Gallic tongue and the Osi's Pannonian show them not to be German, as does the payment of tribute, part to the Sarmatae, part to the Quadi, which is imposed on them as foreigners. though the Cotini, more to their shame, mine iron-ore for weapons. All these tribes possess few flat areas, and mainly occupy the mountain passes and summits. An unbroken range, in fact, divides Suebia, beyond which exist a host of tribes, of the whom the most widespread by name are the Lugii, extending over several states.

It suffices to identify the strongest: the Harii, Helvecones, Manimi, Helisii, and Naharvali. Among the Naharvali a grove is shown, the seat of ancient ritual. A priest in female attire presides, but according to Roman interpretation Castor and Pollux are the gods commemorated there, that is the meaning of the divine powers, named the Alci. There are no images, no signs of imported religion, but as brothers and youths they are venerated.

'Worship in the Sacred Grove'
Reinier Vinkeles, 1788 – 1790
The Rijksmuseum

As for the other tribes, the Harii not only exceed those mentioned in strength but are innately fierce, enhancing their ferocity with art and timing: blackening their shields and dyeing their bodies, they choose dark nights for battle, and awful in the shadows, a deathly army, they bring terror, a novel and hellish vision no enemy dare face, for in every battle defeat first enters through the eyes.

Beyond the Lugii, the Gotones (*Goths*) are ruled a little more tightly than other German tribes, but not yet beyond all sense of liberty. Immediately following, by the coast, are the Rugii and Lemovii: all of these tribes display round shields, short swords, and submissiveness before their kings.

SECTION 44: THE SUINONES

Beyond there, in the very waves themselves, are the territories of the Suiones (Swedes), strong in men, arms and ships. The form of their vessels is unusual, in that a beak at either end is always ready to act as the prow driven forward. They employ neither sails, nor oars in banks at the sides, but paddle freely, as is done on certain rivers, reversing in either direction, as need arises.

Among these peoples, respect is shown to wealth, and in that matter one man rules without exception, his right to being obeyed unchallengeable. Nor is there indiscriminate bearing of arms, as among other Germans, rather they are kept under guard, and by a slave, since the sea inhibits sudden enemy incursion, and armed men without employment easily lend themselves to trouble. Nor is it, indeed, safe for the king to place a nobleman, freeman, or even freedman in charge of the weapons.

SECTION 45: THE AESTII AND SITONES

Beyond the Suiones lies another sea, dense and almost motionless, by which the land is circled and bounded; as shown by the extreme brightness of the declining sun which is so bright as to persist until dawn, dimming the stars: belief also has it that the sound of his rising is heard, and the shapes of his horses and the spikes of his crown are seen. As far as here, rumour proving true, does the natural world extend.

So, to the right-hand coastline of the Suebic Sea (Baltic), that washes the shores of the Aestii peoples, whose manners and dress are Suebic, but whose language is nearer to that of Britain. They worship the mother of the gods. As a mark of their religion they wear the emblem of the wild boar: this rather than armour or human protection renders the follower of the goddess safe even when among enemies. They use swords rarely, clubs more often. Grain and other crops they cultivate with more patience than usual among the lethargic Germans. They harvest the sea too, and they alone gather amber, which they call *glesum* there, in the shallows and along the shore.

Being barbarians, they have not learned or even enquired as to its nature and origin; it lay there disregarded amongst the rest of what the sea ejects, until it found fame among us as a luxury item. To them is appears useless: it is gathered in lumps and sent to Rome unshaped, and they are amazed to receive payment. Yet you may know it is tree-resin, because certain insects, even winged ones, are frequently embedded therein, which caught in its liquid state were later imprisoned there as it hardened. I would suppose therefore that as in the secret places of the East where frankincense and balsam are exuded, so in the lands and islands of the West there are certain fecund glades and groves whose resin is liquefied and, milked by the sun's proximity, oozes into the sea, where storms deposit it on the opposing shores. If you test the nature of amber by setting fire to it, it lights like a torch and supports an oily odorous flame; later melting as if to pitch or resin.

The tribes of the Sitones adjoin those of the Suiones. Similar in other respects, they differ in this, that the women rule: in this respect they are not only inferior to freemen but even to slaves.

SECTION 46: THE PEUCINI, VENETHI, AND FENNI

Here Suebia ends. I doubt whether to count the tribes of the Peucini, Venethi, and Fenni as German or Sarmatian, though the Peucini, whom some call Bastarnae, behave as Germans in language, manners, house, and home. All are dirty, and their chieftains lethargic; degraded somewhat in the manner of Sarmatians, through intermarriage. The Venethi have adopted much of such ways; infesting, as robbers, all the mountains and forests between the tribes of the Peucini and the Fenni.

Yet these peoples may be included among the Germans, since they have fixed abodes, carry shields, and delight in their swiftness on foot: which are all traits distinguishing them from the Sarmatians, who spend their lives in wagons or on horseback.

The Fenni live in a state of amazing savagery, and vile poverty: without armour, horses, or homes; wild plants are their food, animal pelts their clothing, the ground their bed: they place their reliance on bows and arrows, the latter tipped with sharpened bone for lack of iron. This method of hunting supports the women as well as the men; since they freely accompany the men and seek a share of the spoils. Not even their infants have any protection against wild beasts and weather, except the covering of a few woven branches: to these the young return, these are the refuge for old age. Yet they consider this better than groaning over the furrows, labouring at building huts, or involving their own fate with that of their neighbours', in alternating hope and fear. Indifferent to human affairs, indifferent even to the gods above, they have attained that most difficult of states to achieve, they feel no need even for prayer.

All else is the stuff of fables: that the Helusii and Oxiones have the bodies and limbs of beasts, but human faces and features: that, being unknown for certain, I shall leave unresolved.

ABOUT THE AUTHOR

Publius Cornelius Tacitus was born AD56/57, in one of the Roman provinces, possibly Gallia Narbonensis, to an equestrian family. He studied rhetoric in Rome, and in AD77 or 78 he married Julia, the daughter of the noted general Agricola. He held various posts under the Flavian Emperors, surviving the reign of Domitian, an experience which left him with the deep aversion to tyrannical government evident in his writings. He was a Senator, and a Consul *suffectus* in 97 under Nerva, gaining a high reputation as both lawyer and orator. Leaving public life he then turned to literature, though returning to practise law under Trajan. He was a close friend of Pliny the Younger, who assisted him in his early career. His major historical work survives as the *Annals* and the *Histories*, the extant parts of which cover large sections of the period from Tiberius to the death of Nero (the *Annals*, the later work), the Year of the Four Emperors, and the founding of the Flavian dynasty (the *Histories*). In AD112 or 113 he held highest office as civilian Governor of the province of Asia, and may have lived until as late as AD130.

ABOUT THE TRANSLATOR

Anthony Kline lives in England. He graduated in Mathematics from the University of Manchester, and was Chief Information Officer (Systems Director) of a large UK Company, before dedicating himself to his literary work and interests. He was born in 1947. His work consists of translations of poetry; critical works, biographical history with poetry as a central theme; and his own original poetry. He has translated into English from Latin, Ancient Greek, Classical Chinese and the European languages. He also maintains a deep interest in developments in Mathematics and the Sciences.

He continues to write predominantly for the Internet, making all works available in download format, with an added focus on the rapidly developing area of electronic books. His most extensive works are complete translations of Ovid's Metamorphoses and Dante's Divine Comedy.

Made in the USA
Columbia, SC
23 December 2023

29398396R00059